JAMESTOWN PUBLISHERS

TH CONTEMPORARY READER

VOLUME 2, NUMBER 4

JAMESTOWN PUBLISHERS

a division of NTC/CONTEMPORARY PUBLISHING GROUP
Lincolnwood, Illinois USA

ISBN: 0-89061-829-1

Published by Jamestown Publishers,
a division of NTC/Contemporary Publishing Group, Inc.
4255 West Touhy Avenue,
Lincolnwood (Chicago), Illinois, 60646-1975, U.S.A.
© 1998 NTC/Contemporary Publishing Group, Inc..

9 WKT 0 9 8 7 6 5 4 3 2

CONTENTS

Pronunciation Key

ă	mat	o͞o	food
ā	date	o͝o	look
â	bare	ŭ	drum
ä	father	yo͞o	cute
ĕ	wet	û	fur
ē	see	*th*	then
ĭ	tip	th	thin
ī	ice	hw	which
î	pierce	zh	usual
ŏ	hot	ə	alone
ō	no		open
ô	law		pencil
oi	boil		lemon
ou	loud		campus

Josephine Baker
The Toast of Paris

What made Josephine Baker one of the most popular entertainers in history?

1   One of her adopted sons put it bluntly. "My mother," said Jean-Claude Baker, "lived more in one day than most people do in an entire lifetime." That might be an empty boast from most sons. But that was not so in Jean-Claude's case. His mother was the great "Black Venus," Josephine Baker.

Humble Beginning

2   Born in 1906, Josephine started out with nothing. She grew up in St. Louis in "a one-room shack my family called home." Sometimes she had to steal food in order to eat. She wore homemade shoes. She had to grow up fast.

Josephine Baker left behind a life of poverty and racism in the United States to become the toast of Paris during the 1920s.

In her first big show, Josephine played her part for laughs. Her crossed eyes and funny faces made her the star of the chorus.

3   At the age of eight, Josephine went to work. She became a cook and housecleaner for a white woman. It was not a good job. The woman worked her hard and sometimes beat her. She gave Josephine a place to sleep—but it was in the cellar with a dog. Her long hours at work left Josephine little time for school, so she left after the fifth grade.

4   Josephine was still a teenager when her first marriage failed. She left St. Louis for Philadelphia. She wanted a career in show business, so she taught herself to sing and dance. She joined a traveling group called the Dixie Steppers. That gave her experience.

5   She tried another marriage, this time to Willie Baker. It did not last long. She was on her own again, but she kept the name Baker.

6   Then the big break came. Josephine Baker landed a role in the chorus line of *Shuffle Along,* a Broadway musical. She was put at the end of the line, but Baker quickly found a way to call attention to herself. She played her role for laughs. She crossed her eyes, made funny faces, and pretended to be confused. The audience loved it.

On to Paris

7   In 1925, Josephine Baker sailed for Europe. She and 25 other African Americans put on a show in Paris. Baker took the city by storm. French audiences went wild—they simply adored her. And why not? She had everything: style, glamour, and beauty. Baker loved Paris in return. She once said, "Paris is the dance, and I am the dancer."

8 Baker went on to perform in all the great cities of Europe. Famous people were happy just to be seen with her. The author Ernest Hemingway called her "the most beautiful woman there is, there ever was, or ever will be."

9 What made Baker great? She wasn't the best singer of her time, or even the best dancer. But no one put the whole package together as well as Josephine Baker. She knew how to entertain people and make them laugh. Composer and bandleader Duke Ellington once said, "There isn't anything about the stage she doesn't know."

Offstage

10 Baker's life was full of drama offstage as well. In 1939, World War II began. Within a year, the German army had taken over France. Many French people could not accept that, so they formed a resistance[1] movement. It was called the French Underground.

11 Baker joined the movement to help the Americans and their allies. Although her exact role in the movement was not public knowledge, the French honored Baker when the war ended. They gave her the Medal of Resistance.

---

[1] resistance: a secret group struggling against enemy forces that have taken over a country.

Josephine called raising her Rainbow Tribe of orphaned children an "experiment in brotherhood."

12   As an African American, Baker knew about racial prejudice[2]. Some people judged her just by the color of her skin. But Baker did not let that poison her view of the world. She believed that all people could live in peace.

13   For her, these weren't just words: she took action. Baker created what she called her Rainbow Tribe. She and her fourth husband adopted 12 orphans. They came from different races and cultures.

---

[2] prejudice: unfriendly feelings aimed at a person, a group, or a race

14   She worked for peace, but when it came to equality, Josephine Baker was a fighter. During the 1950s, she spoke out for civil rights in the United States. Her words got her into trouble in some circles. As a result, her U.S. shows were canceled.

In her act, Josephine wore wonderful costumes by famous designers. She would make at least seven costume changes per show.

15   Baker had been used to living well, and her expenses stayed high. She lived in a large French country house and had 12 children to support. But she was not making enough money. The cost of it all was just too much. In 1969, she and her family were evicted[3] from the house.

Always a Star

16   Many people would have felt crushed, but not Josephine Baker. She was never down for

---

[3] evicted: forced out by a legal process

long. With help from Princess Grace of Monaco (former actress Grace Kelly) and other friends, she found a new home. She also returned to the stage. By then, Baker was in her sixties, but the old fire and sparkle were still there. She was a smash hit in New York City.

In 1975, Baker went back to Paris. It had been 50 years since she first performed there. She was now 68 years old, and again she conquered[4] [kŏng′kərd] the city. A few days later, a tired but happy Josephine Baker went to bed. She never woke up. She once said of her successful career, "What a wonderful revenge for an ugly duckling."

QUESTIONS
1. What was so hard about Josephine Baker's early life?
2. How did Baker make herself stand out in the chorus line?
3. What qualities made Baker a star?
4. How was Baker's offstage life dramatic?
5. What happened to Baker after she lost her home in 1969?

---

[4] conquered: won over

This is Stonehenge as it looks today. Centuries old,
it remains a symbol of mystery and power.

Mystery
MONUMENT

What is there about Stonehenge that has led people around the world to copy it?

1   *T*o many people, the world's greatest mystery lies in some huge stones near Salisbury, England. These stones form an ancient monument[1] called Stonehenge. The word *Stonehenge* means "hanging stones."

2   Thousands of people from around the world visit Stonehenge each year. Yet Stonehenge has baffled people for centuries. Its stones are arranged in a precise[2] pattern. But no one knows who built the monument or why. Scientists can only guess at the exact dates when it was built.

---

[1] monument: a structure that marks something special
[2] precise: exact

3   At first, people thought that Druids, an ancient group of priests, built Stonehenge as a temple. The Druids, however, did not appear until long after Stonehenge. Other people thought that Stonehenge marked the grave of the famous King Arthur.

The Building of Stonehenge

4   Scientists know that Stonehenge was built in three stages over a long period of time. The first stage occurred[3] about 4,000 years ago. Builders dug a circular ditch more than 300 feet across—which is longer than a football field. Around the inside of the ditch are two more circles, one inside the other. One of the circles is formed by a bank[4] and the other by 56 pits. An avenue passes through a break in these circles. It leads to a massive stone 120 feet outside the circles. This 35-ton stone, called the heel stone, seems to be very important in Stonehenge's design.

5   The second and third stages of construction stretched over the next 200 years. At the center of the outer rings, builders erected a circle of 30 stones. Each stone stands about

---

[3] occurred: happened
[4] bank: a mound, pile, or ridge of earth

15 feet tall. The builders placed 30 more stones across the tops of these to form lintels—like door frames. Inside this stone circle stand five stone structures in a horse-shoe design. Each structure, called a trilithon

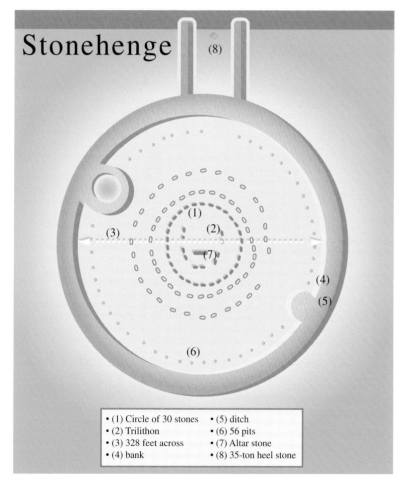

Stonehenge (8)

- (1) Circle of 30 stones
- (2) Trilithon
- (3) 328 feet across
- (4) bank
- (5) ditch
- (6) 56 pits
- (7) Altar stone
- (8) 35-ton heel stone

Many of the monument's stones did not survive the ages. But scholars believe that this was the original plan of Stonehenge.

[trī′lĭth ŏn], has three stones, two standing upright and one lying across them.

6   When people talk about Stonehenge, they are usually referring to the stone circle and horseshoe. Here, huge rocks appear to "hang" over other rocks.

7   The stones forming Stonehenge are huge. Some are 30 feet long and weigh 50 tons apiece. Most came from rock quarries [kwôr′ēz] 20 miles away. But some stones in earlier building stages came from mountains as far as 240 miles away.

The Mysteries of Stonehenge

8   Many mysteries surround Stonehenge. No one knows how the builders, with only simple tools, built such a great monument. They had to move giant stones, smooth their surfaces, and then lift them. To pull a single stone upright required about 200 workers. Also, somehow the builders had to determine[5] the exact positions of the stones.

9   Scientists try to answer these questions: How was Stonehenge built? Who built it? And why?

---

[5] determine: to decide

10   They can only guess what the monument's purpose was. They feel quite sure, however, that it had something to do with astronomy.[6] Stonehenge seems to be a giant sun calendar. On June 21, the longest day of the year, a person can see one way that the calendar works. June 21, called the summer solstice [sŏl′ stĭs], is the day the sun is at its most distant point from the equator. On this day, when the sun rises over the heel stone, the shadow it casts goes directly through the center of the monument. Other stones also seem to be placed in a way that relates[7] to the rising and setting of the sun and moon.

Copies of Stonehenge

11   Some people today are so interested in Stonehenge that they try to imitate it. Many copies exist around the world. There are even several new Stonehenges in the United States.

12   A full-sized copy made of concrete stands on the banks of the Columbia River in Maryhill, Washington. Sam Hill, a successful road builder and businessman, wanted to

---

[6] astronomy: the science of heavenly bodies and their sizes, make-up, and movement

[7] relate: link to

Stonehenge II in Hunt, Texas, is a smaller copy of the original in England. If you pose for photos, be ready to move fast—fire ants are everywhere!

honor 13 local servicemen who had died in World War I. Over an 11-year period, workers poured 1,650 tons of concrete to make Stonehenge I. They even put crumpled tin into the frames when concrete was poured for the pillars.[8] The result was a surface that looked much like that of the original Stonehenge.

13   An architect named Doug Hill built Stonehenge II in Hunt, Texas. With money

---

[8] pillar: a column

and land from rancher Al Sheppard, he made this copy smaller than the original in England. Unfortunately, fire ants have invaded the area. So people are advised to visit the monument during the day to avoid stepping on ant hills.

14   Another copy of Stonehenge sits on the campus of the University of Missouri at Rolla. This monument is made of granite [grăn′ĭt] and, like the original, serves as an accurate[9] calendar based on astronomy.

Funhenges

15   Then there are the funhenges.

16   Take a bunch of beat-up old cars. Stick them in the ground, rear ends up. Lay other beat-up cars across the top. Paint them all gray. And what do you have—Carhenge!

17   In 1987, six families got together to build this so-called monument in Alliance, Nebraska. All were related to Jim Reinders, an engineer who had visited the Cadillac Ranch in Texas. There, between 1949 and 1963, a man stuck 10 of his Cadillacs into the ground, back fins reaching for the sky.

---

[9] accurate: correct

No one would mistake it for the real thing. But Carhenge, a wacky version of Stonehenge, is Alliance, Nebraska's top attraction.

18   Meanwhile, a sculptor named Bill Tishman built a copy of the Nebraska carhenge in Ontario, Canada. The cars in Tishman's "monument," however, are partially crushed. As a result, they are closer in size to the stones of the original Stonehenge.

19   The strangest "henge" of all appeared— and disappeared—in 1994. On a farm near Gordonton, New Zealand, 41 old refrigerators were used to build a fridgehenge. This henge was built to mark the solstice on December 22. The builders mowed a strip

of grass pointing toward the sunrise and used a refrigerator as the heel stone. Before removing the monument, its builders held a huge party, using the refrigerators as musical instruments.

QUESTIONS
1. What does *Stonehenge* mean?
2. Where is the real Stonehenge?
3. How long did it take to build Stonehenge?
4. Why was the Stonehenge in Maryhill, Washington, built?
5. Name two things besides stones that people have used to build henges.

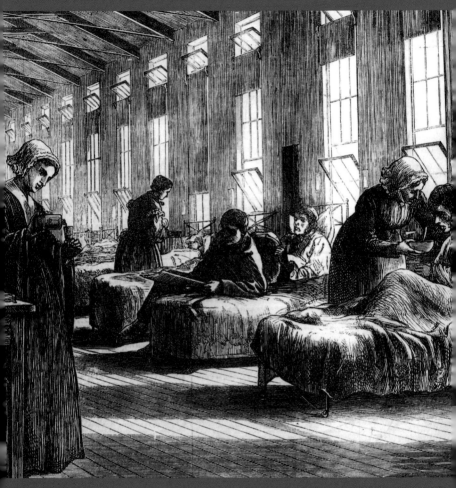

For more than 800 years, people everywhere lived in fear of catching smallpox. Victims were kept away from others, but no real treatment existed for this often-fatal disease.

The Death of SMALLPOX

*How was one of the world's deadliest
diseases wiped out?*

1   There are no smallpox epidemics[1] today.
But smallpox was once one of the great killer
diseases. In all parts of the world, millions of
people—whether peasants[2] or kings—died
from smallpox. A large number of the victims
were children.

2   Writings from A.D. 1241—over 700 years
ago—describe smallpox. But this deadly
disease was probably active for centuries before that time. This is the story of how smallpox was wiped out for good.

---

[1] epidemic: an outbreak of serious illness that spreads fast
[2] peasant: a worker on the land

The Disease in Action

3   A person caught the smallpox virus[3] [vī′rəs] from someone who had the disease. The first sign of smallpox was a very high fever. Then a victim might get a bad headache. Later came muscle pains, backaches, chills, and vomiting.[4]

4   These symptoms could have been the start of many illnesses. But by the fourth day, all doubt was gone. A nasty rash appeared. Hard red lumps popped up on the person's face, hands, and feet. At first, the lumps were filled with a clear fluid. Then the fluid turned to pus as the skin lumps became painful, itchy blisters. These blisters were the "pox" that gave smallpox its name.

5   The blisters soon broke. But they took up to three weeks to form scabs and heal. If a patient lived that long, he or she was often badly scarred. The person had these pock marks, or pits in the skin left by the blisters, for life. Some people who survived were also left blind.

---

[3] virus: an active substance in the body that spreads disease
[4] vomiting: throwing up the contents of the stomach

6   A great number of smallpox victims died. Most often, the cause of death was an infection[5] of the brain, lungs, or heart.

Seeking Safety from Smallpox

7   A person who lived through smallpox could not get this illness again. Having had the disease once built up the body's immune [ĭ myoon'] system.[6] The body was then immune to, or safe from, future attacks of smallpox.

8   Doctors wanted to make people immune to smallpox before they got a fatal case of it. So why not give people a tiny dose of the disease? Once they got well, people would be safe from smallpox forever. Healers in ancient Asia had tried out that idea centuries before. With a needle, they put smallpox pus, taken from a sick person's sores, under the skin. If a patient was lucky, only a mild case of smallpox took hold. A patient who got well was immune for life. But this method, later called inoculation [ĭ nŏk yə lā'shən], was quite risky. Some people got so sick from it that they died.

---

[5] infection: the state produced by a germ or disease

[6] immune system: the body's natural way to fight off disease

9   Even for those who got well, it was a painful time. The patient was kept away from others until the sickness came and went. After that, it often took many weeks for the person to feel well and strong again. Through the years, doctors continued to use the inoculation method. All in all, countries that used inoculation had a lower death count from smallpox than those that did not. Even so, outbreak after outbreak of the disease continued, killing millions.

A New Idea

10   An English doctor named Edward Jenner knew all about inoculation. He had survived smallpox himself as a young boy in the late 1700s. Jenner was a simple country doctor, but he knew a lot about smallpox. He also knew the dangers of giving people a small dose of the disease. Jenner had spent many years looking for a safer way to stop smallpox before it started. In 1796, he found a way to bring the disease under control at last.

Children were hit hard by smallpox. In time, parents began to bring their babies to doctors for Jenner's new method.

11   For much of his life, Jenner had heard farm people say that they could not catch smallpox. They knew it was because they had already had cowpox, a disease much like smallpox. Dairy farmers and those who worked with cattle often caught cowpox. This mild disease of cattle did not kill people or make them very sick. They got a few skin blisters that soon went away. When the workers were later exposed to smallpox, even many times, they did not catch it. Most of these farm workers even refused to be inoculated. They saw no need for it.

Jenner's Vaccine[7] [văk sēn′]

12 Jenner wanted to test out this link between smallpox and cowpox. He tried an experiment. Jenner took pus from a cowpox sore on a patient's finger. He then infected a boy with the pus by putting it into small cuts made on the boy's arm. Jenner then sent the boy home. The boy got cowpox but soon was well again. Then, in a bolder step, Jenner infected the boy again—this time with pus from a smallpox blister.

13   This part of the experiment might have killed the boy, but it didn't. Jenner thought that the cowpox would make the boy's body immune to smallpox. He was right—the boy did not become sick at all from the smallpox pus. Jenner had at last found a safe and simple way to prevent smallpox. He called the pus, or matter taken from the cowpox sore, a *vaccine.* The word comes from *vacca,* which means *cow* in Latin. Jenner called the process itself *vaccination* to set it apart from inoculation. The word vaccination came to mean any process that makes a person immune to a certain disease.

---

[7] vaccine: a mixture containing a virus given to prevent a disease

Smallpox Rages On

14 Jenner's vaccine did not stop smallpox right away. In a world of millions, most people did not get the vaccine. Some did not know about it or could not afford it. Others were afraid of the process. That was true even in the United States. The vaccine first came into use in 1800. But it took about 100 years more before it was widely used.

15 In 1905, the United States Supreme Court took a bold step. It ruled that local boards of health could require vaccination. More and more local boards began to act on that ruling. In 1921, the United States reported more than

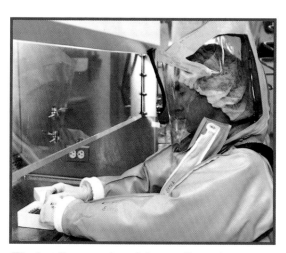

The last live samples of the smallpox virus are kept under close guard by laboratory scientists. Notice the protective clothing this lab worker wears while handling the age-old killer.

100,000 cases of smallpox. Ten years later, the number had dropped to 15,000. The last case in the country was reported in 1949.

The World Scene

16 Smallpox still raged on in other parts of the world. In 1967, the World Health Organization (WHO), a branch of the United Nations, took action. It worked hard to stop the disease everywhere. Slowly, the efforts paid off. The last known case of smallpox was reported in 1979.

17 In 1980, WHO announced the good news: smallpox had been wiped out. No one in the world had to fear it anymore. It is the only natural disease to be so completely conquered.

Death for the Virus?

18 The smallpox virus still exists. Samples of it are kept frozen in two medical research laboratories. One is located in the United States. The other is in Russia. In 1990, WHO voted to destroy even these samples. The great fear is that terrorists might steal the virus and use it in warfare. Most people don't want to take that chance.

19   The virus was to be destroyed in 1993. In the meantime, many science experts argued to save the virus. They wanted more time to study it. The date, reset for 1995, was put off once more because the debate went on. A new deadline, set for 1996, met with further delay.

20   The delays in destroying the virus samples might drag on. But the world waits to see if the killer virus's next date with death—now set for 1999—will be its last.

QUESTIONS
1. What are the symptoms of smallpox?
2. How did healers in ancient Asia try to prevent smallpox?
3. How did Edward Jenner develop a vaccine for smallpox?
4. Why did it take so long for the disease to be wiped out?
5. Why does WHO want the frozen virus samples destroyed?

The Run for the Roses

𝒫

*Which horse was the fastest ever to run
in the Kentucky Derby?*

1 The Kentucky Derby is often called the
most exciting two minutes in sports. It is
held every year in Louisville [lōō′ē vĭl],
Kentucky, on the first Saturday in May. More
than 130,000 fans jam the Churchill Downs
racetrack there to see the Derby. Millions
more watch the race on television. The
audience has one question: Who will win
this year's "Run for the Roses"?

Horse Sense

2 The Kentucky Derby is the most famous
horse race in the United States. Colonel
[kûr′nəl] M. Lewis Clark, a Louisville citizen,

**The Kentucky Derby has been held every year since 1875.
In the background are the famous twin steeple tops of the
Churchill Downs racetrack.**

founded the race in 1875. Clark had studied horse racing in Europe. He was impressed[1] by the racing system and rules used in England and France. Clark modeled his race after the English Derby, a famous race held each year in Epsom, England.

3   Clark hoped to build a strong horse-racing tradition in the United States. But first he had to build his own race course. In 1874, he talked a group of friends into forming the Louisville Jockey Club. Clark must have been a good talker: the new club quickly had 320 members. They each put up $100 to build the track. Clark built the track on a farm owned by a family named Churchill.

4   Clark opened his Kentucky Derby, as he called it, to three-year-old horses only. Both males (colts) and females (fillies) could be entered in the race. But in Derby history, only three fillies have ever won.

The First Race

5   Churchill Downs opened in 1875, the year of the first Derby. The Kentucky Derby was a hit from the start. As a crowd of more than

---

[1] impressed: left with a high regard for something in the mind and memory

Isaac Murphy was one of many African-American jockeys in the Kentucky Derby's early years. He rode Derby horses to victory in 1884, 1890, and 1891.

10,000 fans watched, a horse named Aristides [ăr ĭ stī′ dēz] won the race. The winning jockey was Oliver Lewis, an African American. (Of the 15 jockeys in that first race, 14 were African American.) When the Derby was first set up, horses ran a course of 1½ miles. But in 1896, that distance was shortened to 1¼ miles. That is the length still run today.

6   Clark was only 29 years old when he started the Derby. He earned his place in racing history that day. Over the next 20 years, Clark became the best-known man in Louisville, and his Derby its best-loved event.

The Blue Grass State

7   The state of Kentucky, called the Blue Grass state, has good reason to thank Colonel Clark for the Derby. The race became more and more famous. Many wealthy horse owners and breeders[2] bought large tracts of land in central Kentucky. They built their homes, farms, and horse stables there. The state became the center for racehorse breeding in the United States—and for good reason.

8   The central Kentucky region, known as the Blue Grass, is a rolling, fertile land. The soil there is among the richest in the United States. Loaded with limestone and other minerals, this soil enriches the "bluegrass" that grows on it. Horses feed on the blue-grass, so named for the tiny blue flowers it sprouts in May. These Thoroughbreds[3] grow up strong boned and powerful—perfect for racing. Of the first 121 Derby winners, 91 were bred in Kentucky.

Derby Day: A State-wide Party

9   Over time, the Kentucky Derby grew into something much grander than just a horse

---

[2] breeder: one who raises horses
[3] Thoroughbred: a type of horse bred chiefly for racing

Kentucky, the Blue Grass state, is well known for its racehorse-breeding farms.

race. It became the very symbol of the sport itself. To call the Derby just a horse race is to call the Superbowl just a football game. Like the Superbowl, Derby Day is a spectacle[4] that ranks with such other yearly events as the Indianapolis 500 and the World Series.

10   About 42,000 people fill the grandstands at Churchill Downs. Another 80,000 or so crowd into the infield, or the large oval-shaped space inside the track itself. All kinds of

_____

[4] spectacle: a public show

people come to see the race. The park is packed with plenty of ordinary people. Many celebrities and leaders in business and politics join the fun too. Derby Day is one big party, not just within the park but all over the state of Kentucky. People everywhere go to Derby parties, gathering to watch the race on TV.

It looks close, but jockey Pat Valenzuela (in yellow) took Saturday Silence to the finish line in the 1989 Derby.

The Derby is at the heart of several days of special events and festivals around Louisville.

They're Off!

11   On Derby Day, there are several races on the program at Churchill Downs. Excitement

builds with each one as the crowd gets ready for the final race—the Derby. At last, the Derby horses walk onto the track. As they do, the crowd sings "My Old Kentucky Home," an emotional moment for many. The announcer shouts, "They're off," and the crowd watches history being made. Those who have bet little or nothing cheer as hard as those who bet $10,000 or more on a horse. In just about two minutes, the race is over. Even so, an average crowd feels completely worn out! After loud, long applause from everyone comes perhaps the race's most famous tradition.

A Winning Tradition

12 The winning horse has a blanket of roses draped over its neck. The garland has 500 dark red roses stitched together. No one is sure how the custom started, but it has gone on for more than 100 years. We do, however, know where the Kentucky Derby's nickname "Run for the Roses" came from. A New York sports writer named Bill Corum coined[5] the phrase in 1925.

---

[5] coined: made up

Setting the Record

13   Is the Derby really the most exciting two minutes in sports? Well, not exactly, since one horse *did* finish the race in less than two minutes. The year was 1973, and the horse was Secretariat. He set the Derby record when he ran the race in 1 minute, 59.4 seconds. No other horse has run the race in less than 2 minutes. Secretariat went on to win that year's Triple Crown as well.

The Triple Crown

14   The success of the Kentucky Derby led to the birth of other major U.S. horse races. The Derby is the first of three races for three-year-old horses that make up the Triple Crown. The second is the Preakness, held in Maryland each year in late May. The third race in the series is the Belmont Stakes, run in New York each June. Almost every winner of the Kentucky Derby has gone on to run the next leg[6] of the series, the Preakness.

15   If the same horse wins all three of these races, it has won the Triple Crown. So far,

---

[6] leg: one part or section

only 11 horses have captured[7] this title. Among them were Whirlaway, Secretariat, and Seattle Slew.

16   Year after year, the Kentucky Derby goes on as a beloved American tradition. To many people, it is still just a horse race. Others have visited Churchill Downs to see the Run for the Roses firsthand. They have been a part of this important link to the past. To these defenders of the Derby, no other event can match the "most exciting two minutes in sports."

QUESTIONS

1. Why did M. Lewis Clark want to create the Kentucky Derby?
2. Which horses can run in the Derby? How far do they race today?
3. Why is Kentucky called "the Blue Grass state"?
4. Why is the Kentucky Derby nicknamed the "Run for the Roses"?
5. What is the Triple Crown?

---

[7] captured: won or gained control of, as in a game or contest

Many people claim not to be superstitious, but their actions may speak louder than their words.

A Rabbit's Foot
and a Piece of Wood

Why do people do some of those "funny" things?

1 You sneeze. Someone says, "Bless you."

2 You hiccup. Your friend jumps up and yells, "Boo!"

3 You yawn. Without thinking, you cover your mouth.

4 What triggers[1] such reactions to a sneeze, a hiccup, and a yawn? Actions like these are often a result of customs. Others stem[2] from superstitions [soo pər stĭsh'ənz]. Long ago, for example, many people thought that a sneeze, hiccup, or yawn was the devil at work. So they developed little actions to keep the devil from his mischief.

---

[1] trigger: to set off; cause
[2] stem: to branch or develop from

Customs and Superstitions

5 A custom is the usual way of doing something. A superstition is a belief that one event will cause—or prevent—another event that is in no way related. Customs often grow out of superstitions.

6   Both have been part of every culture in history. But they differ from one culture to another. In Japan, for example, the words for the number 4 and for *death* sound alike. So many Japanese think 4 is unlucky. Some buildings in Japan, therefore, have no fourth floor. In other cultures, people think the number 13 is unlucky.

Many Sources

7 The stories behind superstitions and customs come from many sources.

8   There are at least two stories telling why some people won't walk under ladders. One says that early Christians thought that the triangle formed by a ladder leaning against a building had to do with the Holy Trinity. Walking through a triangle, therefore, meant that a person was working with the devil. Another story says the superstition came from the Egyptians' belief in the power of

This father might be fighting back tears as he "gives the bride away" to her groom.

pyramids and triangles. Nobody should disturb a triangle, they felt.

Fears and Beliefs

9 Customs and superstitions often spring from people's fears and beliefs. They are one way to deal with things people don't understand. Customs and superstitions surround every important thing a person does—eating, sleeping, working, and playing. They also deal with life's major events—birth, marriage, illness, and death.

10   Think of the many superstitions and customs that relate just to marriage:

- A bridegroom carries his bride across the threshold.[3]
- A bride wears something old, something new, something borrowed, and something blue.
- The bridegroom should not see the bride before the ceremony.
- The bride and groom cut the first slice from the wedding cake.

Here is a handful of lucky charms. The plant wrapped in foil is borage, an herb said to drive away sadness and build courage.

- The woman who catches the bride's flowers will be the next one married.
- The man who catches the garter thrown by the bridegroom will be the next to marry.

11   These are just a few of the many customs and superstitions for one event.

Are You Superstitious?

12   Now, do you have a rabbit's foot in your pocket for luck? How about the black cat that

---

[3] threshold: the section of wood or stone that lies under a door

crossed your path? Has it caused a heap of bad luck?

13   Maybe you've already had four years of bad luck because of a mirror you broke. (Take heart! The superstition says the total is seven years of bad luck. So you have only three more to go.) On the other hand, if you were born on a Sunday, you're supposed to have good luck all your life.

14   Do you know why people knock on wood or try to find a horseshoe or a four-leaf clover? Why do people worry when a dog howls? Can you really undo bad luck by throwing some salt over your left shoulder?

15   Each of these superstitions has a story. Most often, there is no way to prove how the story got started. But trying to find out can be fun. See if you can learn why people do some of the things they do.

QUESTIONS

1. What is the difference between a custom and a superstition?
2. Describe one story that tells why some people won't walk under a ladder.
3. Why have customs and superstitions come about?

The promise of land drew wagon trains of settlers westward across the United States.

OUTFITTERS OF THE WEST

*How did two small Missouri towns open up
the great American West?*

1   The year is 1840. You need money and you need it in a hurry. What will most likely bring quick riches?

    A. Go west to Oregon. Start farming.

    B. Go west to California. Pan for gold.

    C. Go to Missouri. Sell supplies to travelers.

2   Your best bet is C. Many merchants did this with great success. They prepared, or outfitted, people who wanted to travel westward on the Oregon Trail. Some merchants were both lucky and greedy. Such outfitters of the West made fortunes in Missouri.

The Louisiana Purchase and Westward Movement

3   Before 1803, the United States reached from the Atlantic Ocean to the Mississippi River. Then the United States bought a huge tract of land from France. This great land deal was the Louisiana [loo e ze ăn'ə] Purchase. The United States instantly doubled in size! The country's land now stretched west to the Rocky Mountains.

4   Two areas lay between the country's new western border and the Pacific Ocean. To the southwest was New Spain. This area included Mexico and what is now Texas, California,

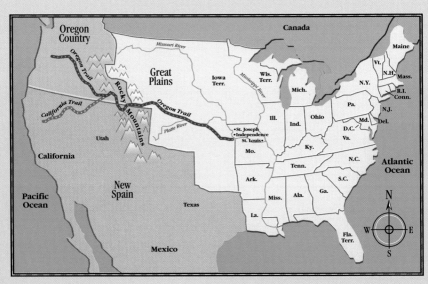

This map shows the region crossed by wagon trains moving westward to Oregon and California.

and the states in between. North of New
Spain was the Oregon Country, claimed by
both the United States and Britain. The
Oregon Country included all of today's states
of Washington, Oregon, Idaho, and parts of
Montana and Wyoming.

5   People soon moved into the land bought
in 1803. But most of them stayed close to
the Mississippi River. By 1820, the states of
Louisiana and Missouri were formed in the
new land.

6   West of the Rockies, reports about the
land along the Pacific Ocean sounded good.
Returning explorers praised the rich farm
land and warm weather of the Oregon
Country. Reports of more good land, forests,
and natural riches in California also called
people westward. Still, few settlers moved
west of Missouri.

Barriers to the West

7   What kept these people from following their
dreams? They faced several barriers. First,
forests and good farm land ended west of
the Mississippi. The weather on the plains
was dry. Farmers had heard that no one
could plow the land there. The roots of the

Store after store opened at the main starting points of the trail to the West. Merchants made a fortune selling goods and services that travelers needed—as well as some they didn't.

prairie[1] [prâr′ē] grass in this region could grow six feet deep. Second, the journey west would be long and hard. The Rocky Mountains are too steep for people and animals to climb. They rise like a huge backbone running north and south. In addition, the mountain winters are very cold and snowy. Even in summer, it is hard to find passes through the Rocky Mountains. Third, California and the Oregon Country were far

---

[1] prairie: flat or rolling grassland

away. Why go farther west when there was
still fine land in nearby Missouri?

8 By 1840, though, Missouri's land was
filling up. Farmers began to think about
the open land in Oregon. Perhaps the long
journey there was worth it, after all.

9 Travelers crossing the prairie would need
water for themselves and for animals. So the
best trail would follow a river. But the river
must not be too deep. A shallow river would
be easy to cross. Of course, the longer the
river was, the better. Luckily, explorers and
traders already knew about such a river.

The Platte River

10 The Platte River begins in the Rocky
Mountains. It flows east across the prairie.
Wagons could cross it easily. One humorous[2]
report said the river is "a thousand miles long
and six inches deep." The Platte finally flows
into the Missouri River. Near the point where
these two rivers meet was the small town of
Independence, Missouri. Next to Independence was its poor neighbor, Westport.
These towns became the jumping-off points
for westbound travelers.

---

[2] humorous: funny

11   The great move westward that began in 1840 was only natural. The first brave settlers bound for Oregon left from Independence. Joel and Mary Walker and their four children were the groundbreakers. They joined a pack train that carried supplies for fur trappers. The group set out on April 30, 1840. The Walkers reached Oregon 136 days later.

12   The next spring, about 60 settlers set out together. They made their way across the prairie and the Rocky Mountains. Then the wagon train split up. About 30 settlers went on to Oregon. The rest turned south to California.

13   With a trail now blazed,[3] travel by wagon train from Missouri boomed. In 1843, about 1,000 people went west. In 1849, gold was found in California. Many miners then went west with the farm families. By 1852, more than 150,000 people had traveled on the Oregon Trail.

Independence and St. Joe

14   About 50 miles upriver of Independence was a small trading post. Its manager, Joseph Robidoux [rō′bĭ dō] heard about the people moving west. He saw the number of these

---

[3] blazed: newly marked or mapped out

Settlers could not do without food for the long trip westward. Grocers gladly sold them what they needed at twice the normal price.

pioneers jump from 6 to 1,000 in a short time. And he acted fast to take part in the boom.

15   Robidoux divided the land around his trading post. He laid out a town and named it St. Joseph. But its nickname, St. Joe, was easier to remember. By 1845, St. Joe was home to almost 700 people. Most of them, especially Robidoux, made a living off people bound for the Trail. The town competed[4] fiercely with Independence.

---

[4] competed: tried to outdo

How Money Was Made

16   Some emigrants[5] to the West Coast came to the two jumping-off towns with their own covered wagons. But many more bought wagons only when they were ready to pack up for the journey. Some wagons needed repairs. Many others needed hoops and canvas covers. In 1849, Independence alone had 20 shops that made and repaired wagons.

17   Another need was for draft animals.[6] Horses could pull wagons fast but not for a long time. Mules could work longer than horses but were harder to handle. Oxen were slow but steady, and they needed little care. Most emigrants chose oxen. Livestock dealers tried to please everyone. They brought horses, mules, and oxen into the towns and sold them quickly.

18   Selling groceries was one of the biggest businesses. Travelers had to carry all their food with them. Each adult needed about 200 pounds of flour and about 75 pounds of bacon. Food prices were quite high in west Missouri. But the merchants charged

---

[5] emigrant: one who moves to a new land to live
[6] draft animals: animals in teams used to pull loads

emigrants twice as much as local towns-
people paid for the same item.

19   Greedy gun dealers also made money.
Native American tribes along the Trail were
usually friendly. But back in Missouri, gun
dealers spread wild tales of tribal attacks.
They sold to scared emigrants guns they
didn't need and couldn't handle. So the emigrants had many gun accidents. They were
more likely to be killed or hurt by gunfire
than by attacks.

20   Even the 11 doctors in St. Joseph over-
charged the emigrants. They set up a system
of fees for common treatments. For a house
call (or wagon call), the doctors charged a
base fee plus a mileage fee. The mileage fee
doubled after dark.

21   Other people in the two towns sold
clothing. Wares also included blankets,
ovens, canoes, and snake oil.[7] Gamblers,
music hall dancers, and saloonkeepers as
well made their share of money off the
emigrants. Each spring, before the wagons
set out, everyone was busy.

---

[7] snake oil: a worthless mixture sold as a cure for many ills

Out for a share of the action, a salesman peddles snake oil to weary travelers.

The Boom Years End

22 The boom years for Independence and St. Joe didn't last long. They reached their peak in 1852. That year alone, about 52,000 people set out on the Oregon Trail. Almost all of them were outfitted in these two Missouri towns.

23 By 1855, other towns were stealing business. Trading posts had sprung up along the Trail. Some clever merchants shipped goods straight through to Oregon or California. Bridges and improved roads shortened the trip westward. Emigrants no longer had to stock up as before. Finally, in 1869, a railroad linked California to the East.

24   Remember little Westport, the neighbor town to Independence? In 1853, it changed its name to the Town of Kansas. It grew and became rich. In 1889, its name changed again—this time to Kansas City. Kansas City kept on growing. In time, it swallowed up Independence. The city of St. Joseph still exists. But like Independence, it is smaller than Kansas City.

25   The towns of Independence and St. Joseph, Missouri, will not be forgotten. They served as doorways to the American West. And their merchants outfitted the pioneers of that vast[8] new land.

QUESTIONS

1. Why didn't farmers rush to claim the prairie land west of Missouri?
2. Why did people want to move west of the Rocky Mountains?
3. Why might a good trail follow the path of a river?
4. Describe three ways in which the merchants of Independence and St. Joe made money off westward travelers.
5. What ended the boom years for Independence and St. Joe?

---

[8] vast: very large

The Bermuda TRIANGLE

Would you set sail for the Devil's Triangle?

1 Hundreds of people are dead. More than 50 boats have sunk, and 20 airplanes have fallen from the sky. Planes are suddenly lost from radar [rā′dâr] screens. The coast guard can find no lifeboats. The navy can find no wreckage[1] [rĕk′ĭj]. Is this the work of a mad scientist? Has a huge comet hit Earth? No, these and other strange events are tied to the mysterious Bermuda [bər myoo′də] Triangle.

Where Is the Bermuda Triangle?

2 The southeast coast of Florida has many visitors. It is a favorite winter vacation area.

---

[1] wreckage: bits and pieces left behind after something has been destroyed

In 1945, five torpedo bombers like these mysteriously vanished in the Bermuda Triangle. No trace of the planes or their crews has ever been found.

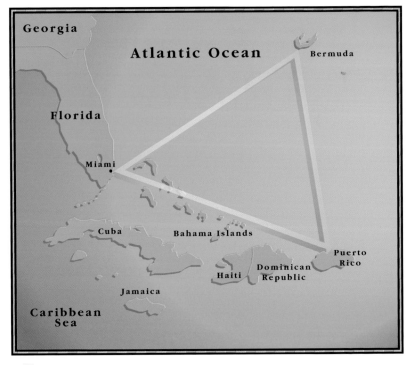

Georgia

Atlantic Ocean   Bermuda

Florida

Miami

Cuba   Bahama Islands

Puerto
Rico

Dominican
Haiti   Republic

Jamaica

Caribbean
Sea

**The Bermuda Triangle is just an area of the Atlantic Ocean.
Yet some people refuse to fly over it or travel within it.**

About 900 miles away, in the Atlantic Ocean,
lies the country of Bermuda. Bermuda is
made up of one large island and many
smaller ones. The weather is warm, and the
land is green and pretty. All year long,
people visit Bermuda. In the Atlantic Ocean,
between the Florida coast and Bermuda, is
the feared Bermuda Triangle.

3   Also called the Devil's Triangle, the
Bermuda Triangle isn't marked on the water.

People don't always agree on its size or shape. But everyone agrees that something is strange about this area of ocean.

Strange Events

4 Here's an example of the mystery. A yacht[2] [yät] leaves Florida, heading northeast for Bermuda. The winds are light. The waters are calm. After two days, there is no word from those aboard the yacht. The United States Coast Guard tries to make radio contact—no answer. A search begins. Ships and planes are on the lookout, but nothing is found.

5 Some people have ideas about the lost yacht. Maybe the cause was a fire on board, a huge wave, or a bad storm. Perhaps the yacht hit another ship. There are many guesses. The official records list the yacht as missing "for reasons unknown."

6 The yacht is only one of many ships that have sunk in the area over the years. In 1840, a French ship named the *Rosalie* was found drifting[3] in the open sea. The ship's crew[4] [kroo] had vanished. A caged canary was the only sign of life aboard.

[2] yacht: a large pleasure boat, most often a sailboat
[3] drifting: moving along without purpose
[4] crew: those who work aboard a ship

Many ships and aircraft have been lost in the Bermuda Triangle. What strange and powerful forces could be at work there?

7   Lost aircraft range from single-engine planes to huge airliners. Perhaps you have heard of Charles Lindbergh, a famous pilot. In 1928, he left the island of Cuba on his way to St. Louis, Missouri. He had to cross the waters near Florida's coast. Some strange things happened on that journey.

8   Lindbergh's compass began turning in wild ways. It moved left, right, slower, faster. Soon it

spun so fast that its face was a blur. Lindbergh had no idea where he was. For a time, he couldn't even see! He said that a mist or a kind of fog closed in around the plane. When Lindbergh later talked about this flight, he said it was like flying through "dark milk."

More Mystery

9 Others who have flown over the same waters weren't as lucky as Lindbergh. In December 1945, five torpedo bombers called "the Avengers" disappeared. The pilots were on a normal training flight when they got lost. They radioed the naval station to report that their compasses were spinning wildly. At the same time, the weather had turned bad. Not only did the pilots lose sight of each other, they also disagreed on their location. Where they were and what really happened remains a mystery. All five planes disappeared. A thorough search revealed nothing—not a single piece of wreckage.

10 John Hawke was a pilot who lived to tell of his experience. Hawke had crossed the ocean many times. But the flight from Florida to Bermuda was almost his last. He talked of seeing a yellow blur. Like Lindbergh and the

bomber pilots, he said the compass needle whipped back and forth. "I felt dizzy. Maybe woozy[5] is a better word, but my balance was slipping away." Hawke passed out, but the plane kept flying on automatic pilot. When Hawke woke up an hour later, the gauges[6] [gāj′əz] showed that the plane had traveled about 400 miles. The way Hawke figured the mileage and fuel usage, such a long distance was not possible. He knew that what happened was beyond explanation.

Some Things We Do Know

11   We do know that the ocean is often quite unpredictable[7] in this area. The fast-moving Gulf Stream, or warm water from the Gulf of Mexico, flows north. Suddenly, it meets the colder and slower main mass of the Atlantic Ocean. As the Gulf Stream forces its way through, there is always a strong disturbance. But sailors know about this danger and are ready for any problems.

-----

[5] woozy: dizzy or weak
[6] gauge: a dial or other instrument that shows airspeed, height, fuel level, and so on
[7] unpredictable: uncertain, not known in advance

12 Hurricanes can cause high waves and choppy waters. But hurricanes give plenty of warning of bad weather. Planes and small boats don't set out in hurricane conditions.

13 Many ships and planes cross this busy region of the Atlantic. Nearly all of them reach land safely. The crews and passengers report nothing odd. Yet the number of boats, planes, and lives lost in the area is higher than it should be—more than can be explained.

14 Of course, if we could explain all the losses, we would have to give up something else. We would lose the awful mystery of the Bermuda Triangle!

QUESTIONS

1. Is the Bermuda Triangle on land or water?
2. Where is the Bermuda Triangle located?
3. How did Charles Lindbergh describe his journey across the Bermuda Triangle?
4. How many miles did pilot John Hawke's gauges show he had traveled?
5. Name two conditions that make the Bermuda Triangle area unpredictable.

The ancient Dead Sea Scrolls were found in these desert caves in Jordan.

SECRETS
FROM THE
DESERT

What are the Dead Sea Scrolls?
Why are they important?

1   It all started with a lively goat. At least, that's the way the story goes.

2   The story comes from a shepherd boy in the Middle East. This boy lived in Jordan. One day, in 1947, he and his goats were out in the desert, near the Dead Sea. One of the goats scampered[1] off. The boy saw it go into a cave. He threw a stone into the cave to

---

[1] scampered: ran in a playful way

scare the goat out. When the stone landed, the boy heard something break.

3   The boy ran off and brought a friend back to the cave. Together they climbed into the dark, dry cave. There they saw what the stone had hit. Lying on the floor were some old pottery jars.

Researchers have a look inside one of the caves.

4   These jars weren't just old— they were ancient. They were 2,000 years old. Rolled up in the jars were some ragged documents[2] as old as the jars.

---

[2] document: a written or printed paper that gives proof of something

5   The boys did not know it then, but the documents were of great importance. They were the first part of the Dead Sea Scrolls [skrōlz]. Later more scrolls and scroll scraps were found in other caves. Researchers and scientists call the Dead Sea Scrolls one of the greatest finds ever.

Important Writings

6   It is not just the age of the scrolls that makes them important. It is what they say. Some of the scrolls and scraps together form the oldest known copies of the Bible. These copies include the books of the Torah[3] [tôr′ə] and most of the other Old Testament books of the Bible.

7   The next oldest copies were made at least 1,000 years after the scrolls. These later copies, written in Latin or Greek, date from the Middle Ages.[4] Only the Dead Sea Scrolls are written mainly in the old Hebrew language.

---

[3] Torah: in the Jewish faith, the first five books of the Bible: Genesis, Exodus, Leviticus, Numbers, and Deuteronomy

[4] Middle Ages: a period in history from about A.D. 500 to A.D. 1450

8   The scrolls date from the time of Jesus. They contain many writings that are not part of the Bible. These writings explain people's thoughts about God and the right way to live. The writers of the first scrolls found were part of a Jewish religious group. Modern scholars call that group the Essenes [es′ ēnz]. They called themselves the Sons of Light.

9   In the scrolls, the Sons of Light told of their beliefs. They wrote down their prayers, songs, and the rules they lived by. As a whole, the scrolls tell much about history and about Jewish beliefs around the time the Christian era began. The scrolls also show clear links between Jewish beliefs and early Christian teachings.

Surviving the Ages

10   It is amazing that the scrolls survived for such a long time. They were written long before paper was invented. People in ancient times wrote on many different materials. Some of the scrolls are papyrus[5] [pə pī′ rəs]. Others are made of leather. One scroll is even made of copper.

---

[5] papyrus: an old form of paper made from a water plant

11   Why didn't the scrolls rot away or just turn to dust? The answer has to do with the weather near the Dead Sea.

12   The land there is very hot and dry. Water never reached the caves where the scrolls were found. Living things need water, so the caves had no forms of life. There was no bacteria[6] [băk tîr′ē ə] to rot the scrolls. They just lay there for hundreds of years, waiting to be found.

Splitting Up the Scrolls

13   For many years after the scrolls were found, scholars had no chance to look at them.

14   The shepherds who found the first seven scrolls sold them to antique [ăn tēk′] dealers. The dealers then sold them to others.

The Dead Sea Scrolls made of papyrus once looked much like this Torah scroll, which dates from a later time.

---

[6] bacteria: germs

Three scrolls were bought for the Hebrew University in Israel. The other four were brought to the United States and put up for sale. In 1954, an ad about them ran in a New York newspaper. A scholar named Yigael Yadin saw the ad and bought the scrolls. He paid $250,000—one-fourth of a million dollars. Yadin then gave the scrolls to the country of Israel.

15   In the meantime, people in Jordan checked other caves near the Dead Sea. They found thousands of scraps from other scrolls. They also found a few more scrolls in fairly good shape. None of these later finds were as important as the first seven scrolls. Still, all of the scraps had great value.

The hot, dry weather near the Dead Sea helped the scrolls survive the ages.

A researcher studies part of a Dead Sea Scroll. The meaning of these writings still causes hot debate among scientists and religious scholars.

Delays

16 Meanwhile, the rest of the world waited. Everyone wanted a look at the Dead Sea Scrolls. But only a few top scholars from around the world were allowed to see them. They said it would take time to read and understand these documents.

17 Years passed. Only the first few scrolls were published. Scholars who were not part of the scroll project got angry. They wanted to know what was taking so long. When would outsiders get to see the scrolls?

Slow Going

18   There were reasons why the work took a long time. One reason was money. A bigger problem was the condition of the scrolls themselves. They were very fragile,[7] so scholars had to work with the scrolls slowly and gently.

19   One scroll remained wrapped up for seven years. Scholars didn't dare unroll it because they feared it would crumble before their eyes.

20   The copper scroll was already broken in two when it was found. Neither half could be unrolled because the old copper was too brittle.[8] Scholars first had to slice the copper into thin strips and then try to read the writing on each strip.

The Scrolls Made Public

21   At last, the rest of the world got to see the Dead Sea Scrolls. For that we can thank Elizabeth Bechtel, a woman from the United States. Bechtel paid to have pictures taken of the Dead Sea Scrolls. In 1991, these pictures were made public.

---

[7] fragile: easily broken
[8] brittle: hard but easy to break

22   By now, many people have had a chance to study the scrolls. But they do not all agree on what the writings mean. Scholars have written books about the scrolls from all points of view.

23   Debate and study of the scrolls goes on. Bit by bit, new findings will help everyone to better understand these treasures from so long ago.

QUESTIONS

1. According to the story, who found the Dead Sea Scrolls?
2. What do the scrolls contain?
3. How did the scrolls survive for 2,000 years?
4. Why has it taken so long for the contents of the scrolls to be known?
5. What finally made it possible for outsiders to study the scrolls?

A Matter of Taste

*What makes a person like some flavors
and hate others?*

1   A favorite flavor hits your tongue. At once, you sense the pleasure of it. The sense of taste is one of life's little treats. Taste also keeps you from eating things that may harm your body. Here is a look at how this special sense does its job.

2   Taste is one of the first senses animals ever had. (The other is the sense of smell.) Billions of years ago, even one-celled animals could taste their food. But pleasure is not the main purpose of taste. A good flavor draws animals to foods that are safe to eat. A bad flavor turns them away from poisons. Even today, this difference helps animals—including humans—know which foods are safe to

It looks as if there's something to suit every taste among the many foods shown here.

eat and which ones will make them sick. It is still important to taste the difference between fresh water and salt water, fresh meat and spoiled meat, and safe plants and deadly ones.

Many Tiny Buds

3   Taste is a chemical [kĕm´ĭ kəl] sense. People sense the chemical makeup of foods through taste buds in the mouth. It's easy to see the little bumps on your tongue. What you can't see are the 100 taste buds on each of those bumps. If you could enlarge a taste bud many times, it would look much like a flower bud. Humans each have about 9,000 taste buds!

4   Most taste buds are on the tongue. However, some may be on the roof of the mouth and in the back of the throat. A baby has more taste buds than an adult has. That's because, unlike adults, babies have taste buds on the insides of the cheeks.

Four Main Flavors

5   Today, there seem to be more and different kinds of foods to choose from. And the creative[1] ways to put these many foods and flavors together are endless. No matter how

---

[1] creative: able to do something in a new way

you combine them, there are only four types of flavors: sweet, sour, bitter, and salty. The taste buds grouped in different parts of the mouth sense each type. Those at the tip of the tongue pick up salty flavors. The taste buds that pick up sweet flavors start at the front of the tongue and end about halfway back. At the back of the tongue are taste buds that sense bitter flavors. Taste buds that tell you something is sour run along the sides of the tongue. The tongue also has special cells that pick up spicy flavors, like hot peppers.

These yummy French pastries could give the taste buds for sweet flavors a good workout!

6   If the tongue and food are dry, there is no taste at all. When you eat, the food mixes with the saliva[2] [sə lī′ və] in your mouth. That mixture "fits" into the right type of taste bud. The taste bud cells that receive the flavor tell the tongue about it. Then nerves in the tongue send word to the brain, which tells you about the flavor.

_____

[2] saliva: water in the mouth that makes chewed food wet

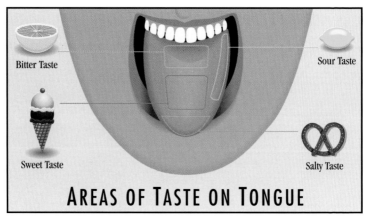

Bitter Taste

Sour Taste

Sweet Taste

Salty Taste

AREAS OF TASTE ON TONGUE

This drawing shows the places on the tongue that sense the four main flavors.

7   The sense of taste in humans is not very strong. It needs help from the sense of smell. As a test, close your eyes and hold your nose shut while putting some food into your mouth. You probably cannot tell the kind of food it is. The need to smell foods is the reason you can't taste them well when you have a cold. Your nose is blocked, so the smell cannot get through to your mouth.

Cooking Up Flavor

8   Most natural flavors come from plants. But plants are not the source of all of the flavors in the foods people eat. Some flavors are made in laboratories for companies to add to the foods they make. Chemists draw a sort of map of a natural flavor. They learn which

chemicals the flavor has. Then they put together the same chemicals to copy the natural flavor.

9   Making a flavor sounds easier than it really is. Most flavors contain hundreds of different chemicals. Only a few of these chemicals give a food its basic flavor. The laboratories must find out which chemicals are important. They get this information by tasting each chemical part of a flavor—something a machine cannot do.

10   Flavors such as vanilla and cherry are easy to make in the laboratory because their chemistry is fairly simple. But flavors such as coffee and chocolate are not easy to make. They have perhaps 800 or 1,000 different chemicals that need sorting out. And for a flavor to seem true, the smell must be right too.

11   Some popular flavors are completely made up. The flavor in a cola drink is not the same as that of a cola nut. Many times, a made-up flavor tastes better than the real thing. Taste tests show that people often prefer[3] the made-up flavor because it is stronger. This is true of orange, the world's favorite flavor. In a test given by the U.S. Army, people chose

---

[3] prefer: like better

made-up orange juice over fresh-squeezed. People say that they want their food to be "all natural." But they also want it to have a good, strong taste. Getting a taste that satisfies might mean adding flavor made at a laboratory.

Could this little guy's flavor mix be a bit heavy on the peas?

Who Likes What

12   Everyone likes a sweet taste more than a bitter one. But why do some people like one flavor and not another? People in one part of the world might love spicy foods while people living elsewhere can't stand them. No one is born with a liking for certain flavors. Instead, a person learns to like what he or she is fed as a baby. So it is natural to be afraid of new flavors. This basic fear explains why a baby's parents might mix applesauce into a meal of mashed peas. In each new mix, the parent uses less applesauce. Little by little, the baby learns to like the flavor of peas.

13   People have to get used to certain flavors. For example, it takes time to learn to

like spicy foods. For very young children in Mexico or Asia, hot peppers cause pain in the mouth. But by age five or six, the youngsters have learned to love them.

14 Does the sense of taste fade in humans as they grow old? It's true that older people have fewer taste buds, but not fewer enough to make a difference. Some older people, however, do have less of a sense of *smell*. Their food may not taste as strong as before because their sense of smell has weakened. These people might enjoy some of the stronger flavors made in a laboratory. In any case, the sense of taste brings too much joy to give it up without a fight!

Q U E S T I O N S

1. How does the sense of taste protect the body?
2. Which basic flavors can people taste?
3. Why is it hard for a person with a cold to taste food?
4. Why do people often like made-up flavors better than natural ones?
5. How do people grow to like certain foods better than others?

Players can choose from several games in a state lottery.

The Scoop on Lotteries

*How can a state lottery
make you a sure winner?*

1   Megabucks. Lotto. Powerball. The Big Game. By some name, a lottery goes on close to you. Almost every state has one. Most have daily games called Pick 3 and Pick 4. They have many other lottery games too. In all, there are hundreds of games in the United States. Not long ago, there were no state lotteries. Today that is hard to believe.

No Sure Thing

2   A lottery is a form of gambling. Players bet a small sum of money. In return, they get a chance to win a large sum

of money. Lotteries are based on chance—no skill is involved. That makes lotteries different from picking the win- ner of a contest.

3   A lottery is based on picking random[1] numbers. The payoff is based on the odds. What is the chance of picking the right number or numbers? The higher the odds are, the higher the payoff will be.

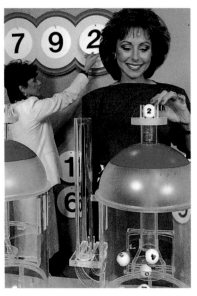

Even in lottery games with a small payoff, the odds are always against the player.

4   Look at the daily Pick 3. You pick a number between 000 and 999. One number in a thousand is right. If you pick it, you win. A $1 bet might bring $500.

5   In Pick 4, the right number is between 0000 and 9999. You have just one chance

---

[1] random: without a pattern

in 10,000 of winning. Pick 4 is harder to win than Pick 3, so the payoff is higher. A $1 Pick 4 bet might win $5,000 or more.

6   The odds are always against you. But in big-money games, the odds are incredible[2] [ĭn krĕd′ ə bəl]. Each lottery is a bit different, but the main idea is the same. The game might be to pick six numbers out of forty. The odds of choosing the winning numbers are several million to one! The payoffs, of course, are also huge. Many jackpots are worth more than $5 million.

A Voluntary Tax

7   The lottery is a kind of "voluntary[3] tax." No one has to pay this "tax." If you don't like the game, you don't have to play. The sure winners are the people who never play. They let the gamblers pay this "tax."

The Lottery in History

8   Lotteries go back a long way. The Bible has stories of dividing land by drawing lots.[4] Roman emperors used lotteries to entertain

---

[2]incredible: not believable
[3]voluntary: by one's free will
[4]lot: an object used in making a choice at random

people. The prizes were often slaves or property. In the 1500s, lotteries became popular in Europe. Governments used them to raise money. Italy's lottery of 1530 was the first to offer prize money. France and England also used lotteries.

9 In United States history, the lottery goes way back to colonial [kə lō′ nē əl] times. Lotteries raised money for public works. The profits from them paved roads and built wharves.[5] Lotteries also paid for buildings at Harvard, Yale, and other fine schools.

Backlash Against Lotteries

10 Lotteries lost favor during the 1800s. Too often they were corrupt,[6] so laws were passed to ban them. England got rid of its lottery in 1826. France did the same ten years later.

11 Churches led the fight against lotteries in the United States. Church leaders said that lotteries hurt the poor. Most rich people don't play the games,

---

[5] wharf: a place to unload a ship
[6] corrupt: dishonest through and through

Would you have guessed that lottery money helped build a school like Harvard?

but poor people want the chance to strike it rich.

12   One state after another outlawed lotteries. Only Louisiana ran one. But by the end of the 1800s, it died there too. Many leaders thought that lotteries were bad for people. The United States Supreme Court said that lotteries were demoralizing[7] [dǐ mor′ ə līz ǐng]. Congress agreed and made it illegal to sell lottery tickets by mail.

---

[7]demoralizing: leading people to do bad things

Another Chance

13   Times have changed again. Today, people don't think gambling is so bad. They again see lotteries as a way to raise money. (Most states keep about half of the money raised. They give back the rest in the form of cash prizes.)

14   In 1963, New Hampshire started its own lottery. It was the first legal state lottery in nearly a century. It was so popular that people from other states drove to New Hampshire to buy tickets.

15   As a result, other states were not happy. They did not like money flowing to New Hampshire, so they began their own lotteries. Lottery fever spread. By 1990, 42 states plus the District of Columbia had lotteries. The games made more than $20 billion!

16   Some say that too much lottery money comes from poor people. But states like the extra income. It's hard to turn down so much cash. For the present, it seems that lotteries are here to stay. ◆

QUESTIONS

1. What is a lottery?
2. Why do some games pay more than others?
3. Why did people once outlaw lotteries?
4. How is a lottery a form of voluntary tax?
5. Why are lotteries back?

PHOTO CREDITS

Cover M. Cunningham. **vi** AP Photo. **2** Corbis-Bettmann.
5 UPI/Corbis-Bettmann. **6** UPI/Corbis-Bettmann. **8, 9** Rob
Talbot/Tony Stone Images. **14** Texas State Department of
Tourism. **16** Nebraska Department of Economic Development.
18 Hulton Getty/Tony Stone Images. **23** The Image Bank.
25 Center for Disease Control. **28** Churchill Downs
Incorporated. **31** Keeneland Library. **33** © Gary Cralle/ The
Image Bank. **34** UPI/Corbis-Bettmann. **38** ©Will Crocker/The
Image Bank. **41** Kaluzny/Thatcher/Tony Stone Images. **42** John
Turner/Tony Stone Images. **44** UPI/Corbis-Bettmann.
48 Corbis-Bettmann. **51** UPI/Corbis-Bettmann. **54** The Image
Bank. **56** Hulton Getty/Tony Stone Images. **60** Everett Johnson/
Tony Stone Images. **64, 65** © Don Smetzer/ Tony Stone
Images. **66** Hulton Getty/Tony Stone Images. **69** Hulton
Getty/Tony Stone Images **70** © Don Smetzer/ Tony Stone
Images. **71** Hulton Getty/Tony Stone Images. **74** Charles
Thatcher/Tony Stone Images. **77** © Charles Gupton/Tony Stone
Images. **80** G. Gladstone/The Image Bank. **82** © David Woods/
The Stock Market. **84** © Roy Morsch/The Stock Market.
87 © Hiroyuki Matsumoto/Tony Stone Images.

Illustrations Mitch Lopata